About this book

This book has been produced to stimulate young children into discussing their surroundings. Each photograph has many elements about which a child should be encouraged to talk. The simple text is only a basis for discussion - a starting point from which to further explore.

Helen Barden

A typeface with a special purpose

The typeface used in this book, Sassoon Primary, was created especially for children by Dr Rosemary Sassoon, a leading educational expert. Exhaustive research with teachers and children resulted in the creation of a typeface which uses child-orientated letters that combine friendliness with functional legibility. The combination of long ascenders and descenders, exit strokes and increased letter spacing, improves the reading quality of the text and also helps children progress towards an efficient, mature handwriting.

YOUNG EXPLORERS

PARK

Helen Barden & Chris Fairclough

Franklin Watts
London/New York/Sydney/Toronto

Designed and produced by
SQUARE BOOK COMPANY
32 Smithbrook Kilns
Cranleigh, Surrey GU6 8JJ
England

First published in 1992 in Great Britain by
FRANKLIN WATTS
96 Leonard Street
London EC2A 4RH

FRANKLIN WATTS AUSTRALIA
14 Mars Road
Lane Cove
New South Wales 2066

ISBN 0 7496 0868 4

Designed by Bridget Howland and Bob Northover
Photographs: Chris Fairclough Colour Library
Printed in Malaysia

A CIP catalogue record for this book
is available from the British Library

Do you like going to the park?
What do you like doing there?

It is fun to go on the swings with your friends.

Or maybe you enjoy feeding the ducks and swans.

Some parks have beautiful gardens...

and others have boating lakes as well.

There is lots of safe space to ride a skateboard...

or race your bike as fast as you can.

There is lots to play on in the park.
You can go up on the see-saw...

and down on the slide.

Are you good at climbing?

Dogs like to play in the park too.
Do you have a dog to play with?

This gardener works in the park.
He is planting out some bulbs in a flower bed.

Look how beautiful they are when they flower.
How many different colours can you see here?

Parks usually have many different trees.
This is a horse chestnut tree.

Have you ever collected horse chestnuts?

Maybe you have had a picnic in the park with your school...

or with your family.

This man is *feeding* the pigeons.

But this squirrel likes to find his own food.
What do you think he is eating?

Lots of people play games in the park.
These boys are playing football...

and these girls are playing tennis.

Look at all this litter!

Take care of your park.
Help keep it clean and tidy.